READING POWER

Biomes

Grasslands

Holly Cefrey

The Rosen Publishing Group's
PowerKids Press™
New York

Published in 2003 by The Rosen Publishing Group, Inc.
29 East 21st Street, New York, NY 10010

Copyright © 2003 by The Rosen Publishing Group, Inc.

First Edition

Book Design: Mindy Liu

Photo Credits: Cover © Bohemian Nomad Picturemakers/Corbis; pp. 4–5 ©
Tom Bean/Corbis; p. 5 (top) Mindy Liu; p. 6 © Paul A. Souders/
Corbis; pp. 7, 16, 17 © W. Perry Conway/Corbis; pp. 8–9
© Anup Shah/Animals Animals; p. 9 (inset) © Gallo Images/Corbis;
pp. 11, 13 © Richard Hamilton Smith/Corbis; p. 12 © Tom Edwards/
Animals Animals; pp. 14–15 © Wally McNamee/Corbis; p. 18 © John
Moss/Photo Researchers, Inc.; p. 19 © Corbis; pp. 20–21 © Tom
Nebbia/Corbis; p. 21 (inset) © James P. Jackson/Photo Researchers, Inc.

Library of Congress Cataloging-in-Publication Data

Cefrey, Holly.
Grasslands / Holly Cefrey.
   p. cm. — (Biomes)
Includes bibliographical references.
Summary: Describes the different types of grasslands, including
savannahs, steppes, and temperate grasslands, and examines their
ecosystems.
ISBN 0-8239-6457-4 (lib. bdg.)
1. Grassland ecology—Juvenile literature. 2. Grasslands—Juvenile
literature. [1. Grasslands. 2. Grassland ecology. 3. Ecology.] I.
Title. .
QH541.5.P7 C39 2003
577.4—dc21

                                    2002002927

Contents

Grasslands

Grassland is land that has few trees and is covered mostly with grass. There are two types of grasslands—tropical and temperate. The grassland biome is usually found between the desert and the forest biomes. Grasslands cover over one-quarter of Earth's land surface and are found on all continents except Antarctica.

Now You Know

A biome *(BY-ohm)* is a plant and animal community that covers a large part of the earth.

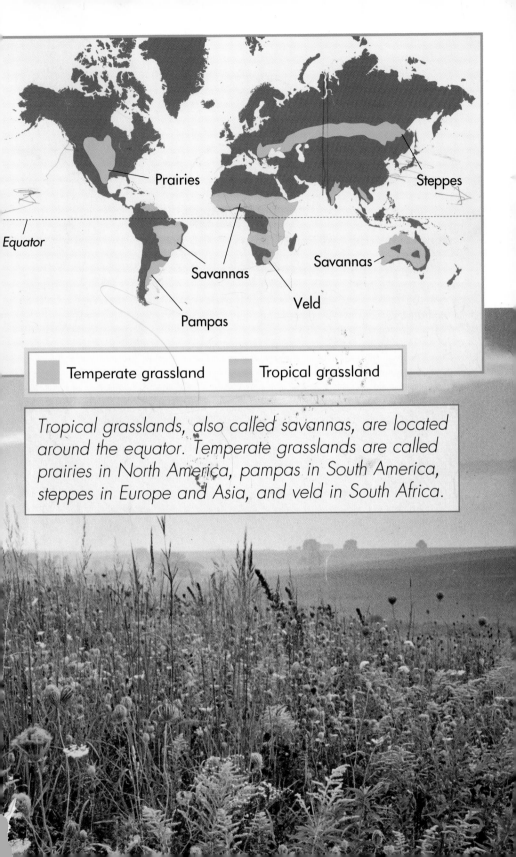

Prairies

Steppes

Equator

Savannas

Savannas

Veld

Pampas

Temperate grassland   Tropical grassland

Tropical grasslands, also called savannas, are located around the equator. Temperate grasslands are called prairies in North America, pampas in South America, steppes in Europe and Asia, and veld in South Africa.

Tropical Grasslands

Tropical grasslands, or savannas, are found in Africa, Australia, South America, and India. The weather is hot all year long. Many animals make their home in savannas around the world. Some of these animals include elephants, lions, kangaroos, termites, snakes, and beetles.

Kangaroos live in the Australian savanna.

6

Many large, plant-eating animals, such as elephants, live in the African savanna.

Now You Know

Savannas cover more than two-fifths of Africa.

Savannas have wet and dry seasons. Some trees and shrubs grow in these grasslands. Savannas get from 10 to 60 inches of rain a year. Dry seasons can last five months or more. During dry seasons, there are many brushfires that destroy the savannas' trees but not the grasses.

The grass in a savanna grows back after a brushfire. Savanna grasses have long roots that live through fires. As soon as it rains, the grasses start to grow.

Some trees in savannas can be found growing on termite mounds.

Temperate Grasslands

Temperate grasslands are found in parts of North America, South America, Asia, and Africa. Temperate grasslands are usually flat with very few trees. They can have very hot summers and very cold winters.

Early pioneers called the American prairies "seas of grass."

Prairies are temperate grasslands that have tall grasses and few trees. Prairies usually have rich soil and receive 20 to 35 inches of rain a year. Very few natural prairies remain today. Most prairie land has been turned into farms or used for feeding animals.

Prairie dogs are members of the squirrel family. They live in large, underground communities in the prairies of the western United States.

Many flowers grow in temperate grasslands. These include asters, blazing stars (pictured below), coneflowers, goldenrods, sunflowers, and wild indigos.

13

Steppes are temperate grasslands that have short grasses and no trees. These are dry areas that receive only 10 to 20 inches of rain a year. Most steppe plants usually grow less than one foot high. People grow wheat and other crops in this temperate grassland. Also, they let livestock feed on the plants and grasses.

This cowherder's cattle feed on the grass of the steppes in Russia.

15

Animals that live on steppes must be able to live without much water. Animals, such as ground squirrels and ferrets, feed on plant life. Other animals, such as bobcats, hawks, and snakes, feed on smaller animals and insects.

Different kinds of animals live in different grasslands of the world. This burrowing owl lives in North American grasslands in holes no longer used by the animals that dug them.

Bobcats usually come out at night. They live in the temperate grasslands of North America, as well as in other biomes.

Now You Know

The people of Mongolia use horses as their main means of travel on the steppes.

Living in Grasslands

Many people live in the grassland biome. Farmers can grow many crops in the grasslands' rich soils. Some people who live in grasslands move around from place to place to farm and to raise animals.

People living in the Cameroon grassland in western Africa use rich grassland soil to grow crops such as maize, yams, and peanuts.

More than two-thirds of the people in Argentina live on the pampas. They use these grasslands for farming and feeding livestock.

The world's grasslands are in danger of disappearing. Many grasslands have been turned into farmland or have been used up by animals feeding on the grass. Grasslands are very important to humans so they must be cared for and respected.

When grassland is turned into farmland, there can be problems. Without the roots of the grasses to keep the soil in place, the soil gets blown away.

Efforts to save the grassland in the United States include replanting grass where it was cleared for farming. When left alone, the new grass helps turn farmland back into grassland.

Glossary

continent (**kahn**-tuh-nuhnt) one of the seven great masses of land on Earth

equator (ih-**kway**-tuhr) a make-believe line around the center of the earth

pampas (**pam**-puhz) grasslands that are found in South America

plain (**playn**) a large, flat, open area of land

prairies (**prair**-eez) a large area of flat land that is covered with grass and has few or no trees

savanna (suh-**van**-uh) a grassland that has scattered trees and shrubs

steppe (**stehp**) one of the large grasslands in parts of Europe and Asia that has no trees

temperate (**tehm**-puhr-iht) neither hot nor cold

termites (**ter**-myts) very small antlike animals with soft, pale bodies; they live in large social groups

tropical (**trahp**-uh-kuhl) of the tropics, which are the hottest and wettest parts of Earth

veld (**vehlt**) grassland found in southern Africa, that has scattered trees or shrubs

Resources

Books

Grassland
by Edward R. Ricciuti
Benchmark Books (1996)

Grasslands
by Darlene R. Stille
Children's Press (2000)

Web Sites

Due to the changing nature of Internet links, PowerKids Press has developed an online list of Web sites related to the subjects of this book. This site is updated regularly. Please use this link to access the list:

http://www.powerkidslinks.com/bio/grs/

Index

Word Count: 440

Note to Librarians, Teachers, and Parents

If reading is a challenge, Reading Power is a solution! Reading Power is perfect for readers who want high-interest subject matter at an accessible reading level. These fact-filled, photo-illustrated books are designed for readers who want straightforward vocabulary, engaging topics, and a manageable reading experience. With clear picture/text correspondence, leveled Reading Power books put the reader in charge. Now readers have the power to get the information they want and the skills they need in a user-friendly format.

A NOTE ON THE TYPE

The text of this book was set in Electra, a typeface designed by W. A. Dwiggins (1880–1956). This face cannot be classified as either modern or old style. It is not based on any historical model, nor does it echo any particular period or style. It avoids the extreme contrasts between thick and thin elements that mark most modern faces, and it attempts to give a feeling of fluidity, power, and speed.

Composed by North Market Street Graphics,
Lancaster, Pennsylvania

Printed and bound by Berryville Graphics,
Berryville, Virginia

Designed by Virginia Tan

A NOTE ABOUT THE AUTHOR

Marcia Bartusiak is an award-winning author whose previous books include *Through a Universe Darkly, Thursday's Universe, Einstein's Unfinished Symphony,* and *Archives of the Universe.* Her work has appeared in such publications as *National Geographic, Smithsonian, Discover, The New York Times,* and *The Washington Post.* She teaches at MIT and lives in Sudbury, Massachusetts.